Guy Fawkes: The Gunpowder Plot

Written by Maureen Appleton

Contents

CHAPTER 1 - The Seeds of Treason

Many nations have some special day upon which the people celebrate a particularly outstanding event in their country's history. In France, the anniversary of the fall of the Bastille is the occasion for a holiday with great public rejoicing. In the United States, Independence Day is celebrated, and the people remember the historic moment when their nation began its separate existence. In England, the one special day of the year when we light bonfires and let off fireworks is November the Fifth, a day when, for the last three and a half centuries, Englishmen have burned Guy Fawkes in effigy and have celebrated with a profusion of rockets, Roman candles and noisy squibs. It is a day on which a good many people are likely to injure themselves and a great deal of property will be damaged, but this is regarded as of small account amidst so much natural jubilation and thanksgiving.

Other nations are celebrating some great event in their history: some turning point in their destiny. In England we are celebrating something which did not happen; and that may seem strange. It is even stranger that some writers go so far as to say that there was not really any plot at all. It is also notable that the man we burn year after year was not the main author of the Gunpowder Plot, though, as we shall see, there were good reasons why it was Guy Fawkes who became the villain in popular imagination.

How truly there was a real plot we shall have to judge for ourselves as the tense story unfolds; but it is not to be wondered at that Englishmen felt a shock of horror and of relief from catastrophe on November 5, 1605, or that we still celebrate the deliverance. Men, who were themselves good, in the sense that they were filled with religious zeal, had certainly planned one of the most evil deeds in history. They had planned murder on a mass scale; murder of King and Lords and Commons, in one single, instant act of hideous destruction.

To us it is hard to believe that good men, with a burning sense of idealism, should have contemplated such an act, whether or not they were deliberately tempted. If we want to understand how it came about, we must make an effort to think ourselves into the state of mind of men in the early seventeenth century; to imagine what it was like when religion was the most important thing in men's lives, and when to hold the wrong views about it led to persecution, and perhaps to cruel death.

It would be quite wrong for us to suppose that religious intolerance has now disappeared. It has not; there are cases of it every day, though fewer in England than in many other countries. On the other hand, we no longer burn one another at the stake at Smithfield for worshipping in a manner that goes against official policy. An Englishman's religious beliefs are, very rightly, regarded as his own business.

Parliament House, Westminster Hall and the Abbey, based on a contemporary print

This was emphatically not so in the seventeenth century, and to understand the temper of the times we can think about the beliefs for which our own generation has been prepared to suffer and die. To be a Roman Catholic in a Protestant country, or vice versa, was as dangerous and frightening then as it was to be a Jew in Hitler's Germany. It was a great deal worse than having a skin of the wrong colour in a country where racialism, either white or black, is rampant. Men will always be willing to die for their passionate beliefs; it is those passionate beliefs which change, not the nature of men.

Since it had been founded, there had always been quarrels in the Christian Church, and some of them had shaken the later Roman Empire. But, for five hundred years, the greater part of Europe had had one Church, the Catholic Church, under one head, the Pope. Though there had been minor fallings away, it must have seemed to most people in Western Europe that the Catholic Church was the rock upon which their society was founded. At the beginning of the sixteenth century men were wakening to the new learning and new ideas, which we call the Renaissance, and began to question more effectively than they had done before the evil practices which had grown up around the Church and to question its teaching. Others had done this before; but, in Martin Luther, a champion arose who challenged the Pope, and who succeeded in founding a new Church in Germany. A little later, Calvin, in Geneva, carried what became known as the Protestant movement still further.

This rebellion against religious authority, which is known as the Reformation, resulted in wars and turmoil. Families were set against one another; parents were divided from their children. Men took religious arguments very seriously, and thousands were martyred for their faith. In England, where the break with the Catholic Church had been less violent and sudden than in many countries, the Reformation still divided the people.

It would take many pages to go into details about this period of turmoil and strife, and all we can do here is to stress that it was the repercussions in England which set the stage for the Gunpowder Plot. The general situation created a climate of opinion in which suspicion and fear were rife, and in which fact and fantasy became so intermixed that we cannot now sort out the strands of plot and counter-plot, or separate hard facts from rumours and deliberate fabrications.

The main entrance to the former Whitehall Palace

The English people have always been regarded as of independent mind, but in this particular case they were content to follow any strong lead. To some extent, this may have been because there was no sudden, complete Reformation in England. Henry VIII took the first steps, for purely selfish reasons; reduced to its essentials, he found it convenient to make his own rules as Head of the Church rather than obey the orders of the Pope in Rome.

Henry VIII, who helped to lay the first stones of the Reformation in England

Henry is one of history's oddities. He is often remembered as "Bluff King Hal", and it is probably true that he remained popular with the mass of the people all through his reign, despite the undeniable fact that he was one of the most cruel, grasping and unprincipled monarchs that the English have ever had to endure. He met with surprisingly little opposition when he decided upon a break with Rome. A few notable persons objected, and were predictably executed (Sir Thomas More being the best known), but there was no nationwide protest. Henry, as usual, had his own way.

By his own wish, he was succeeded by his son Edward VI, who had been brought up as an extreme Protestant. During his short reign the Church in England was taken a long way down the road of Reformation, but he died in 1553, and his place was taken by Mary, a bigoted and fanatical Catholic.

Philip II of Spain

Mary married the Catholic champion, Philip II of Spain, and set out to bring England back into the Roman camp. There followed the infamous Marian persecution, with Protestant martyrs being burned at the stake at Smithfield. This was hardly calculated to increase the Queen's popularity, but one must not fall into the error of supposing that Mary's throne was rocked because of the persecution itself. By the time she died, in 1558, her position had been greatly weakened, but this was because of quite different events-the unpopularity of the Spanish alliance, in particular, and the futile war with France. And then came "Good Queen Bess", Elizabeth 1. To suggest that Elizabeth's character was flawless would be a gross distortion of the truth. She was far from flawless, as she showed on a good many occasions. Yet by the standards of her time, she was tolerant; she burned few heretics, and those mainly for political reasons. The Church which was emerging was a compromise, neither wholly one thing nor wholly the other. The Church of England has been described, not unfairly, as having a Protestant doctrine and a Catholic liturgy. Elizabeth was not a bigot, and did not encourage bigotry; but without any intention, her brand of Christianity became associated in the minds of her people with national pride and national survival.

Elizabeth I, during whose reign national pride outweighed religious intolerance

This was partly because Elizabeth herself was so popular. She stimulated English chivalry, and English greatness came to be linked with her person. This was even more evident because England became engaged in a bitter life-or-death struggle with the power of Spain. The war was in no small measure a religious conflict; Philip of Spain had many mundane reasons for wishing to subjugate England, but at the same time he regarded himself as the Catholic spearhead, and with the backing of the Pope he sought to depose her more-or-less Protestant sovereign. All that was evil, all that was dangerous became synonymous in English eyes with the hated name of Spain-and, therefore, of Roman Catholicism.

Another reason for fear and misgivings in England was uncertainty about the future. Elizabeth had no direct heir, and at that period of history there was no clear or formal right of succession to the throne. The person who seemed to have the best probable claim was Mary Stuart, better remembered as Mary Queen of Scots. Her character was, to put it mildly, disreputable; she was a fanatical Catholic, and widow of the Catholic King of France. It became unsafe for her to stay in Scotland and she had taken refuge in England, where for many years she was half refugee and half prisoner.

Elizabeth was in an extremely difficult position so far as Mary was concerned. All those who were bigoted Catholics, or who had other grounds for detesting Elizabeth, would have been glad to see Mary on the throne, and plot followed plot, the general idea being to bring in troops from either France or Spain. As long as Mary lived, Elizabeth's life was precarious. At last the matter was settled. Mary allowed herself to become entangled in one plot too many, and Elizabeth's hand was to all intents and purposes forced. It was the so-called Babington Plot which was the direct cause of Mary's trial and execution, and this in turn finally drove Philip of Spain to unleash the Armada against England.

Robert Cecil, the First Earl of Salisbury, and Chief Minister to Elizabeth I and James I

It may seem unnecessary to go into details of the Babington Plot in a book dealing with 'gunpowder treason', but the two are closely linked. The Gunpowder Plot came in a different reign, but it was really only one more in the series of conspiracies which had threatened the life of Elizabeth and the security of England. Moreover, there were similarities in the Government's handling of the two affairs. Note, incidentally, that while the

Gunpowder Plot is surrounded by mysteries and uncertainties, the Babington episode was much more clear-cut, and it provides what may be regarded as a significant dress rehearsal.

Anthony Babington was a young Catholic gentleman who became acquainted with Mary's agents in France, and undertook a plot to assassinate Elizabeth, liberate Mary, and conquer England with the help of a foreign army. That Babington really intended to do all this is beyond question. It is also beyond question that Walsingham and the elder Cecil, Elizabeth's ministers, knew all about the conspiracy from the beginning, and encouraged it for all they were worth, so that they could spring the trap at the appropriate moment. They even organized the secret "postal system" by which Babington corresponded with Mary.

Sir Francis Walsingham

From their point of view, Mary was a danger to their country and to their sovereign. They saw it as their duty to find evidence sufficient to remove her, and one can appreciate their attitude even if one disapproves of it. Whether they actually egged Babington on, or whether they merely kept his clumsy treason under close review, is a matter of opinion. What can hardly be disputed is that Mary herself was a willing participant in the whole scheme.

Rather strangely, some historians argue that Mary was blameless because the plot was always known to the Government. Yet so far as either moral or legal guilt is concerned, this contention is indefensible. Mary knew that there was murder and treason afoot; she was more than ready to approve of it and encourage it. We may think Walsingham and Cecil odious and dishonest, but that makes Mary's conduct no less so. The point is worth labouring here, because the same argument has been used about the perpetrators of the Gunpowder Plot. Can we really claim that the plotters were innocent simply because the authorities knew exactly what was happening?

There is one other point to be noted. In the Babington case, it is fairly certain that either Cecil or Walsingham caused a postscript to be forged to one of Mary's letters. The postscript was not intended to increase or reveal Mary's guilt, in spite of what some historians say; she had made her guilt clear enough in any case. The postscript was meant to show up the names of Babington's accomplices, and in fact he was arrested before he had had time to answer the letter. The whole episode is important because it shows that the Government was not above a little helpful forgery, and forgery is sometimes hinted at in connection with documents in the Gunpowder Plot.

This has been a long introduction to the subject, but the story is quite incomprehensible without a clear understanding of the background of the time. The Gunpowder Plot was only one of a series of plots, which cannot make sense unless looked at as a whole.

CHAPTER 2 – Enter King James

WHEN at last Elizabeth's long reign came to a close with her death in 1603, none of the threatened and feared calamities came about. James VI of Scotland, son of Mary Stuart, came quietly to the English throne as James I. That there was no stir, no threat of opposition, may have been chiefly because so many people expected so many things of him. Without wishing to be unkind, one cannot disguise the fact that James was so anxious for the throne of the larger kingdom that he was prepared to go to almost any lengths to obtain it. He had accepted his own mother's imprisonment and execution with no more than a formal protest, and although it is fairly certain that he had made rash promises of toleration for the Roman Catholics, which the people of England would not have accepted, it is probable that he did not even favour these personally.

Be that as it may, it is quite certain that English Catholics had high hopes of better treatment, and were prepared to give James at least a provisional welcome; after all, the new King's mother had been a Catholic, even though the King himself was not. This mood of optimism did not last long. Though Elizabeth had been clement by nature as well as by policy, it would not have been practicable at that time to allow complete religious freedom. Acts had been passed restricting the freedom of Catholics and subjecting them to severe penalties. These measures were renewed soon after the accession of James. In the temper of the country, it would have been virtually impossible to do anything else.

One particular aspect of Elizabeth's policy had considerable bearing on the story of the Gunpowder Plot. Priests were regarded as more dangerous than Catholic laymen, but special hatred was reserved for the Jesuit fathers. They were regarded-often with excellent reason I-as agents of foreign powers who wanted to overthrow England by bringing in foreign armies. For this reason, they were detested by the mass of the people, and were officially persecuted.

The Jesuits of this period have earned a sinister reputation, which some of them deserved. Their name has become a byword for verbal trickery, and "Jesuitical" is still a synonym for equivocation. On the other hand it has to be remembered that the members of the Society of Jesus have left the world in their debt for much that is best in human conduct.

Many of them were willing and faithful martyrs for the faith in which they believed so passionately, and they also did fine work in promoting the best kind of education. Since that time, too, they have contributed much to the advancement of learning.

Mary Queen of Scots

The Jesuits of James I's age were cunning and ruthless, but they were also courageous and scholarly. In trying to work out how far the Jesuits were involved in the plots of the time, some historians pay too little attention to the change in policy which the Papacy (and to some extent the Jesuits too) had followed with James's accession to the throne. So long as Mary Queen of Scots had lived, there had been an open and clear-cut way of changing the national religion of England; all that had to be done was to murder Elizabeth and then land a foreign army on English soil. With James, the position altered radically. He had two sons, both of whom were being brought up as Protestants; James's death would merely transfer power to a boy under the tutelage of the younger Cecil, an arch-enemy of Catholicism. Therefore, Papal policy shifted from the hope of murder or invasion to one of seeking to obtain concessions. It is not at all certain that the Jesuits of 1605, considered as a body, wanted or were likely to help in the violent schemes which had appeared to be desirable only a short time before. It is not difficult to see the cause of Catholic despair and frustration. They had had their hopes raised; almost at once these hopes were dashed, and the effect was profound. James had been barely established on the throne when some of the more eager and hot-headed English Catholics, who may well have been unduly optimistic, were cast into profound dejection by the discovery that James's promises were worthless and that their lot was to remain unaltered. True, the Pope and the many English Catholics who had always been loyal to the Crown might have been willing to practise patience and bide their time. On the other hand, some of the young, eager fanatics were only too willing to revert to violence-and that on a scale which made Babington's futile plotting appear as mere child's play.

In offering a short history of the plot which followed, it is difficult to know where to begin, because every "fact" has been contested, and there is no agreement at all on even the bare outline of what took place. Perhaps it will be best to start with the story as it was set out in the official account of the plot, drawing partly on the confession of Thomas Winter, one of the alleged conspirators-though the confession is itself suspect. Later we can look at some of the contradictions, and examine the rival theories which have been advanced. As a preliminary, however, we must say something about the main actors. They were men of different characters and abilities, which is one reason, though by no means the only one, why the plot failed so completely.

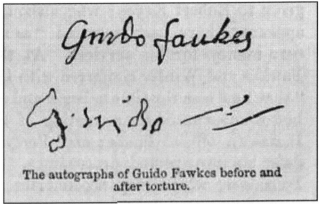

The autographs of Guido Fawkes before and after torture.

An impression of Guy Fawkes' signature, as recorded on a State document

CHAPTER 3 – The Plotters

To some extent, the Gunpowder plot was a local conspiracy. There were in the Midlands a number of Catholic gentry, many of whom were closely related to one another, and who were restless and ready for desperate measures. Into the plot, however, they introduced others of their friends and relatives, including three who came originally from York.

Of these, the most famous by name is Guy Fawkes. Though, as we shall see, he came later into the conspiracy, circumstances led to his being the plotter whose name has come down in history. Guy Fawkes, who spelt his name in a variety of different ways, as did many people in those days, is sometimes called Guy, Guido or Guydo Fawkes, or Faukes. He came of a family less aristocratic than most of his companions, his father having been an ecclesiastical notary, and one of his great grandfathers having been a Lord Mayor of York, whose daughter left to Guy her best whistle and an angel in gold. They were a well-to-do family, and Guy inherited property from his father. Though an uncle left his money to Guy's sisters he bequeathed to Guy "My gold rynge and my bedd and one payre of shetes with th'appurtenances".

Guy went to school at the Free School of York, where were also two other subsequent plotters, John and Christopher Wright. He was educated as a Protestant; but, when his father died, his mother married Dionis Baynbrigge, a gentleman who was related to many members of the Catholic aristocracy. It is probable that, in his new home at Scotton in Yorkshire, Guy became a fanatical Catholic. At any rate, shortly after he came of age, he disposed of his father's property and went as a soldier of fortune in the Spanish army in Flanders, which was then a refuge for the more adventurous Catholic exiles.

In this service, Guy achieved some distinction. He was present when Calais was captured, and earned a reputation for nobility and virtue. At least we may be sure that he was a man brave beyond the ordinary and firm in his beliefs-whatever we may think of his principles. On the death of Queen Elizabeth, he was sent, together with Christopher Wright to Spain by Sir William Stanley, an English renegade in the Spanish service. The object of the journey was to seek help in the task of overthrowing the English government and setting up a Catholic state.

Ashby St. Leger, where Catesby lived with his mother after selling the family estate

At that period, though there were many Catholics in England, there was never any chance of a Catholic revolution without help from abroad, from either France or Spain. All plots had at their roots the hope of some such help, though there was never any chance of getting it, nor of hope for its success even if it had materialized.

The old hall at Scotton, where Fawkes spent part of his youth

With his background of military experience and fanatical religious views, it is not surprising that the originators of the plot sought out Guy Fawkes when they needed a bold and resolute man, who was not well known by sight in England. Though, as we have said, he was not the originator of the plot, he was a man well equipped to play a leading part.

The dubious honour of being the chief organizer must go to Robert Catesby, a Catholic from an old Warwickshire family. Without Catesby there would have been no plot at all, and without his force and energy the plans would certainly have been abandoned at a fairly early stage. Like so many men of the time, he was a curious mixture. He was brave, strong and persuasive, but at the same time reckless, unscrupulous and cruel.

During Elizabeth's reign, Catesby had been involved in the Earl of Essex's abortive rebellion. Since other members of the plot had also been implicated, it is reasonable to look for some connection between the two treasons. As Essex himself was an ardent Protestant the link is not easy to see. Perhaps one can say no more than that the earlier event showed a readiness on the part of the plotters to resort to violence without any clearly thought out object in view. They were restless and daring, but astonishingly muddle-headed.

Though Catesby had been forced to sell his family estate, he contrived to avoid more serious trouble. In this, he was more fortunate or more cunning than his father, who had seen the insides of many prisons because of his Catholic faith. His winning manner and handsome face were assets that he used to the best possible effect. He was of the type who believed that he could always "talk himself out of a scrape", and in his earlier days this seemed to be true. Certainly it was difficult to cajole some of the other plotters into a scheme for mass murder, but Catesby succeeded in doing so. He himself had no scruples at all, and he was able to stifle the consciences of his colleagues. The one mitigating fact is that he was apparently sincere in his Catholicism, and genuinely thought that in blowing up King and Parliament he would be rendering England a service.

Coughton, the home of a Roman Catholic family related to Catesby and Tresham

All through the preparations Catesby took the lead; it was he, of course, who selected the team. Thomas Winter was an early recruit. He was an expert linguist, and had undertaken a secret Jesuit mission in Spain, so that he was no beginner in duplicity. He was also a good soldier, and a man of considerable all-round ability, so that Catesby found him invaluable. Between them, Catesby and Thomas Winter managed to draw in Robert Winter, Thomas's elder brother, but with indifferent success; Robert Winter was always luke-warm, and backed out as soon as he could, though not in time to save himself from being put to death.

Of the rest, we need say little. There was John Wright and his brother Christopher; taciturn, fierce John Grant; Ambrose Rookewood, who was a devoted Catholic, but who would never have become involved in anything so sordid as the Gunpowder Plot but for the winning ways of Catesby; and Robert Keyes, who was "sober and stern", and as fanatical as converts from one religion to another usually are. Sir Everard Digby, like Rookewood, might have been expected to be too cultured and far-sighted to be drawn in by Catesby or anyone else, particularly as King James had knighted him in the previous year, but he too agreed to play a part. Thomas Percy was of different stamp. Like various other members of the conspiracy, he had been involved in the Essex affair, and he was dishonest and aggressive as well as unscrupulous. His unpopularity might well have made him a source of danger to the plotters, but Catesby was anxious to recruit him because of his position in Court; it was he who managed to obtain the use of the vault which became so essential a factor in the operation. Francis Tresham, who can best be described as a crafty villain, was invited to join the plot because he was extremely rich, and considerable sums of money would obviously be needed. Such were the men who plotted Gunpowder Treason. Now let us see just how they set about it.

Robert Winter's house at Huddington

CHAPTER 4 – The Plot Thickens

I the spring of 1604, Thomas Winter was staying at his brother's house, Huddington in Worcestershire. He had been ill, and was depressed and unhappy to the point where he was thinking of emigrating to the Continent. A message was brought to him urging him to come up to London, where his friend Robert Catesby was eagerly awaiting him. Winter refused; but a second and even more pressing summons came, and he yielded.

On arrival at Lambeth, he found Catesby in conference with his cousin John Wright, and it was now that he was first told of the plot which Catesby and Wright were hatching. Whatever one may think of Catesby's ethics or wisdom, there can be no doubt that he was a man of immense charm and strong character. Re seemed to have the power to persuade men of normally sound sense and honesty to plunge headlong into the most dangerous and foolish enterprises.
He told Winter that he had worked out a plan to overthrow the Government and open the way for a Catholic revival. The plan was at least simple, if breathtaking in its folly and callousness.

It was no less than to blow up the House of Lords at the time of the re-opening of Parliament, when the King, together with his elder son Prince Henry, the Ministers and many ambassadors, together with the whole House of Lords and House of Commons, could be destroyed by one huge act of mass murder.

A discussion taking place among the conspirators

Even Catesby's charm could not instantly blind Thomas Winter to the many absurdities of the suggestion, quite apart from any natural shrinking from so terrible a deed. Winter pointed out that such an act would do no more than cause general chaos; it would hardly allow power to fall into the hands of a small group of traitors. Probably he also pointed out that it would be impossible to carry the plan through without being discovered, and that they must either destroy their friends together with their enemies or else warn a substantial number of Catholic peers, in which case the secret would be impossible to keep.

To some extent, Catesby overcame Winter's scruples and sense. He urged that the evils from which the Catholics suffered had originated in Parliament, and that it would be only poetic justice to make Parliament the scene of a gigantic act of revenge. He insisted that only some desperate deed could restore a desperate situation. In the end, it was agreed that one more effort should be made to secure relief by less violent means. Winter undertook to go over to the Continent and interview the Constable of Castile, Philip of Spain's emissary at the peace talks which were taking place with the English. If promises of help were forthcoming, then the plot could be shelved. If not, then the plot must go forward.

Winter duly made the journey. Though the Constable spoke fair words, Winter felt, quite rightly, that no help could be expected from that quarter. English Catholics had long looked to Spain as the one source of help, but now it seemed that the coming peace would end even that possibility, and so Winter's journey must have served to increase the sense of bitterness and frustration common to all the prospective plotters. At any rate, Winter returned from Brussels committed to the Catesby remedy. With him he brought Guy Fawkes, who was apparently enthusiastic from the outset.

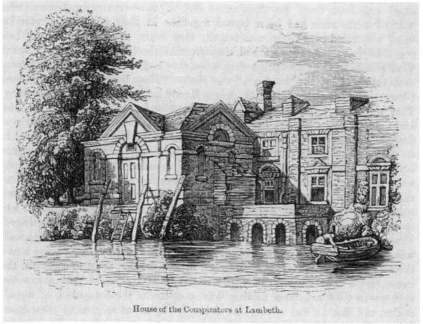

House of the Conspirators at Lambeth.

The conspirators' house at Lambeth, where the plot was first discussed

As soon as he arrived back in England, Winter again met Catesby and Wright and introduced Fawkes. To the meeting also came Thomas Percy, a fairly distant cousin of the powerful Earl of Northumberland, for whom he acted as agent on the family estates. There is some doubt as to whether Percy had been sent for, or whether he merely happened to turn up at the critical moment, but at any rate he seemed to be exactly the right sort of material. On meeting the others, he is said to have exclaimed bitterly: "Shall we always, gentlemen, talk and never do anything?" Catesby was able to answer him at once with a promise of action drastic enough to satisfy even Percy. It was at this moment that the plot was officially born. The five men decided that they would commit themselves to the enterprise, and took the most binding oath not to betray each other in the event of discovery, after which they took Communion together. This was administered to them by the Jesuit Father Gerard.

Father Garnet

Later, and indeed ever since, it has been a matter of dispute how far, if at all, the Jesuits were party to the plot. At least it is undeniable that three Jesuits, Fathers Garnet and Tesimond as well as Gerard, were closely associated with the plotters, whilst no non-Jesuit priest seems to have had any close contact with them. The plotters themselves denied that Father Gerard had any knowledge of the purpose of the meeting.

The plot now began to gather momentum. Even while Winter had been abroad, Catesby had been trying to overcome one of the main practical problems-the lack of a suitable base for operations. He had found that there was a house next to the House of Lords which might be available for hire, and Percy, using the connections he had through the Earl of Northumberland, set out to rent it. He was successful, and Guy Fawkes was installed there, using the name of Johnson and passing himself off as Percy's servant.

Percy's lodgings next to the House of Lords

In one way it seemed that Providence was on the side of the conspirators. To dig a mine from the hired house and extend it under the House of Lords was no small undertaking. In fact, it proved impossible-that is to say, if it were ever attempted.

The story runs that it was tried, but the traces never seem to have been discovered afterwards. At any rate, time would have been all too short; but fortunately, if one may use the word, the opening of Parliament was postponed in what proved to be the first of a series of delays. It is worth noting at this point, that by tradition the Commons always joined the Lords for the opening ceremony in the Lords' chamber.

The mine had to be dug by people quite unused to this sort of work. Guy Fawkes, the only one who may have had some experience of mining operations in war, was employed as look-out, and the others found themselves faced by a wall many feet thick. They began work in December 1604; Parliament was expected to meet in February. It must have been a relief when the date was postponed to the following October.

While these operations were proceeding slowly and painfully, a start was made in collecting gunpowder in the Lambeth house belonging to Catesby. Robert Keyes, a new recruit, was put in charge of the house and store. Another newcomer was Christopher, brother of John Wright.

The problem of digging a tunnel looked formidable. Fortunately the conspirators had a stroke of luck. They learned that a coal merchant, who hired the vaults immediately under the House of Lords, was giving up his tenancy. Percy immediately set about renting the vaults himself. In this he was successful, so that the conspirators were provided with an ideal place for laying their mine without any digging. It must have looked as though Providence was on their side. As we shall see later, there can be some doubt whether it was Providence at work, or a more human and hostile agency!

Meanwhile, the conspirators were perfecting their plot. The mere blowing-up of the King and House could be no more than a curtain-raiser, however dramatic, to the seizing of power. The first thought of any traitor at that time was, of course, to enlist foreign aid. With the peace between England and Spain, this conventional project looked very dubious, but it was almost second nature for the plotters to apply. More negotiations took place, though without much real hope of success. In addition, some rather more practical ideas were canvassed.

It was not at all certain that Charles, James's younger son later to become King Charles I-would be at the ceremony, .and it was necessary to make plans to seize him. This task was assigned to Percy. As a Gentleman Pensioner, he had access to Charles, and planned to introduce enough confederates to overpower any resistance at a time when so many people would be absent at the House of Lords.

Another essential part of the plan was to abduct the Princess Elizabeth, James's daughter who later married the Elector Palatine and became the tragic Queen of Bohemia. She would be staying in Warwickshire, and a hunting party was to be organized as an excuse for collecting a large crowd of Catholic gentlemen on the spot. When she had been seized, she was to be proclaimed Queen, and a Government was to be set up in her name.

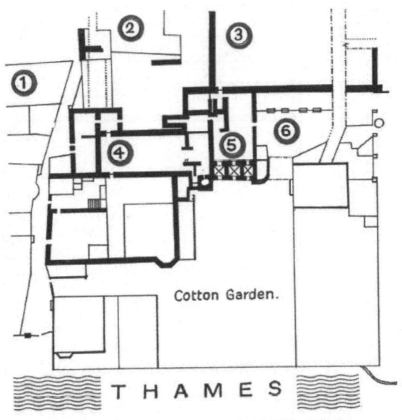

A Plan of Parliament, showing the position of Guy Fawkes' cellar

1. Star and Garter public house
2. Modern front
3. The present House of Lords, formerly the Court of Requests
4. Guy Fawkes' cellar under the old House of Lords
5. Cellar under the Painted Chamber
6. Site of the old Cloisters

The plotters seem to have laboured under the delusion that as soon as the standard of revolt had been raised, they would at once be joined by the majority of the Catholic gentry. Even if this had been likely (which in fact it was not) they would hardly have made much headway, but in any case the very idea shows that they were completely out of touch with reality.

Some of the conspirators at least, notably Thomas Winter, ought surely to have had more sense.

The numbers of people involved had already become too large for safety. Apart from Fawkes, they were all men who were under suspicion, and who were probably watched almost continuously. Every extra member added to the danger.

Nevertheless, the numbers were increased still more. For one thing, it was essential to have more financial help, since up to that time all the costs had been met by Catesby. Percy was ready to rob his kinsman and employer, the Earl of Northumberland, of some thousands of pounds, but even this was hardly enough. Robert Winter and John Grant were enrolled on Easter Day, March 31, 1605, and at about the same time there came Ambrose Rookewood, who was a man of considerable wealth, and who owned a stable of fast horses; he rented Clopton Hall, near Stratford-on-Avon, which would be very handy when the moment came to start the revolt, especially if the plot were to fail. In addition to these, Thomas Bates, Catesby's devoted servant, had also become aware of the plot-as he could hardly help doing-and was officially admitted to it.

The introduction of these new members had not been unattended by difficulties. Rookewood, especially, was revolted by the idea of wholesale slaughter, and it was not easy for Catesby to overcome his misgivings. This brought a new danger.

It would have been unthinkable that so many men, not all of them bad in their true natures, could have carried out the deed without heart-searching and, one after another, they wished to warn various friends among the potential victims. Catesby, the most ruthless of the group, constantly promised that various means would be used to keep away those Catholics whose lives ought to be saved. How this could have been done without raising suspicion was never made clear, and, ostensibly at least, it was a warning which finally proved the ruin of the plotters.

One argument that Catesby used to deaden the consciences of his fellows was his claim that the Jesuits-in particular their leader in England, Father Garnet, had approved the action in principle. This was probably untrue, but it does seem that Catesby had a talk with Garnet in which he put a hypothetical question: "If there is no other means of redress of wrongs imposed, is it not right to take life, including the lives of friends?" He received a reply which he believed gave him justification.

The position of the Jesuits in the whole affair remains dubious, but it appears that Catesby confessed the whole plot to Father Tesimond under the seal of the confessional, and that Tesimond passed it on to Garnet also under the seal of the confessional. Almost everyone, including Anglicans, accepted that such confidences could not be broken under any circumstances whatsoever, even when wholesale murder was afoot.

The position must have been undoubtedly difficult for the Jesuits. Apart from what they knew from under the seal of the confessional, they can hardly have failed to realize that something drastic was being planned. It is hard to doubt that they could have killed the plot quickly if they had really wanted to do so, without technically breaking their duty of secrecy. However, they did not-and the plot went on. Because of the delay in the opening of Parliament, events largely marked time through the summer of 1605. Some new arms were bought for use in the planned revolt, and the Wrights, who lived in Yorkshire, moved down to Warwickshire to be near the centre of operations when the time came. In August, a group met at Bath, and decided to increase the number of conspirators still further.

In a foolish moment, the last two recruits were enrolled. The first was Sir Everard Digby, a man of considerable charm and with a good position in the world. The second was Francis

Tresham, brother-in-law to Lord Monteagle-one of the nobles of the Court-and cousin to Catesby and Winter.

Tresham's character does not seem to have been estimable. He had been an unsatisfactory son, and was constantly in debt; he appears to have been thoroughly unstable. With Monteagle, he had been involved in the Essex rebellion, and had been approached by Cecil with a view to being used as a spy. There is some suspicion that he did, in fact, play this role.

According to his own account, he remonstrated violently with Catesby when told the details of the plot, and there are reasons for thinking that he was at best half-hearted about it. More forcefully even than the others he wanted to warn his friends, particularly Lord Monteagle. In all probability, Catesby regretted his action almost as soon as he had taken Tresham into the plot.

CHAPTER 5 – Discovery and Disaster

As the date for the assembling of Parliament drew closer, the disputes and scruples within the group multiplied Catesby must have been busy and harassed with the task of over persuading his companions and arguing away their misgivings. It is fairly certain that in doing this he exaggerated, if he did not directly invent, the moral support that he claimed to have drawn from his discussion with Father Garnet.

Arguments raged about who was to be kept away from Parliament, and how it was to be done. Catesby had the sense to see that a warning would be tantamount to publishing the whole story in public. He claimed that by various methods, some of the Lords could be kept away, and suggested, for instance, that Lord Arundel, a very senior Catholic peer, whom all the plotters wanted to save, could be made to undergo "a slight accident". Others, he said, would in any case be absentees. It did not sound very convincing.

Some of these talks took place in London, while at other times the plotters met at White Webbs, a house belonging to Ann Vaux, a devout Catholic who had long been a follower and disciple of Father Garnet. In fact, her house was the Jesuit headquarters in England, which provides yet another of the many links between the Jesuits and the plotters.

It has never been made clear just who was to be saved, or how this could be done without revealing the whole plot. However, it is not at all surprising that the plot finally came to light-officially, at least-because of a warning contained in an anonymous letter.

At this point, interest shifts to Lord Monteagle. He had been a Catholic, and, as we have seen, had taken part in the Essex rebellion. He had also been in collusion with others, at an earlier time, in trying to secure Spanish help in previous plots. He had told King James that he had given up the Catholic faith, but whether or not he had actually done so must remain an open question.

Lord Monteagle

On the evening of Saturday, October 16, Monteagle had taken a sudden decision to move to his house at Hoxton. While he was at dinner, a letter was brought in which had been handed to a footman by a mysterious stranger. Finding, or pretending to find-that the letter was almost illegible; he handed it to one of his henchmen, Thomas Ward, and told him to read it aloud.

Ward then read out one of the most famous and puzzling letters in history. It was unsigned, and was worded as follows:

my lord out of the love i beare to some of youere frends i have a eaer of youere preservacion therfor i would advyse yowe as yowe tender youer lyf to devyse some excuse to shift of youer attendance at this parleament for god and man hathe concurred to punishe the wickedness of this tyme and thinke not slightlye of this advertisment but retyere youre self into yoire countri wheare yowe maye expext the even in safti for thowghe the are be no appearance of ani stir yet I say they shall receyve a terrible blowe this parleament and yet they shall not seie who hurrts them this councel is not to be contemned because it maye do yowe good and can do yowe no harme for the dangere is passed as soon as yowe have burnt the letter and i hope god will give yowe the grace to mak good use of it to whose holy protection I commend yowe.

Monteagle took the letter seriously enough to hurry off immediately with it to Cecil. It was late at night by then, but Cecil lost no time in consulting some of his colleagues. They decided that it should be shown to the King, who was due to return on October 3I from Royston, where he had been staying.

In the meantime, perhaps not unnaturally, news reached the plotters that the secret was out. Since Ward was a friend of many of them, this is hardly surprising, though we have no direct evidence of who carried the news. Winter says that on Sunday night, "one came to my chamber and told me that a letter had been given to my Lord Monteagle to this effect, that he wished his lordship's absence from Parliament because a blow would there be given, which letter he presently carried to my lord of Salisbury" (i.e. Cecil). Next day, Winter went to White Webbs and told Catesby that they were discovered.

James I, who interrogated Fawkes at Whitehall Palace

If the author of the anonymous letter had thought that the warning would make the conspirators
abandon their plot and fly for safety, he had grossly miscalculated. Catesby and Fawkes, at least, were made of sterner stuff. Catesby refused to budge; he decided to stay put, and await developments. When nothing much seemed to happen, he came to the conclusion that the warning had not been taken seriously, or else had not been understood. Fawkes, with a coolness and courage worthy of a better cause, stayed where he was.

*Here is the very lantern Guy Fawkes was caught holding while
unloading the explosives he planned to blow up the house of
parliament with on the Fifth of November.*

When the King returned, he was duly shown the letter. Cecil
believed, or pretended to believe, that the letter was a hoax, but
the King took a more serious view. When Cecil pointed out the
strange wording, "For the danger is past as soon as you have
burned this letter", James (no doubt with a superior smile)
explained that the writer meant only that the danger would be
swift. One might, he said, read it as: "The danger will be past as
swiftly as this letter would burn in the fire."

One can scarcely avoid smiling at the idea that Cecil was not
able to interpret an obscure phrase as easily as the King.
Neither does the wording fit easily into James's interpretation.
For the matter of that, no one, for all the study that the letter
has received down the ages, has offered any really plausible
explanation of what the words were really meant to mean. After
discussion, it was decided that a quick search should be made
of the Parliament building, though it should be delayed until the
eve of the sitting so as to give any possible conspirators every
opportunity to put their mine in place. The search would be
carried out by the Lord Chamberlain, as would be normal for
him at the time.
In due course the Chamberlain carried out his inspection, and
reported that the vault was piled high with fuel which belonged
to Percy. He suggested that there was far more of it than would
seem to be needed for Percy's own use, and that it might easily
conceal powder) He also observed Percy's "servant" standing
by, coolly watching the proceedings.

As soon as he heard that the vault was rented by Percy,
Monteagle had misgivings; he knew his kinsman's weakness
for becoming mixed up in plots. Cecil and the King felt that
there was sufficient cause to go further into the matter, and they
decided that a thorough investigation should be carried out that

evening by a magistrate. The reluctance with which the decision was taken is difficult to understand, whatever one believes about the plot. If Cecil really knew all about it, all he had to do was to close the jaws of the trap which he had laid; the pantomime would be pointless and meaningless. If he did not know about it, then why did he hesitate? His ostensible reason was that it would only create alarm and despondency if a furore were raised and proved to be unfounded. Yet since the job could be (and was) done without any publicity, this argument too is weak.

The search was carried out at night. Whatever may have, been known or guessed about the plot it must have been a moment of tense excitement and drama. We can picture many hands tearing at the heaps of fuel in the yellow, flaring light of torches. First the stave off a barrel must have come to sight, and then, in rapid succession, barrel after barrel crammed with powder-everyone sufficient to send the searchers to a searing and sudden death. Together, that great store might have reduced the whole solid fabric of the Palace of Westminster to a heap of blackened rubble. With it might have gone the King in his jewelled crown, the nobles in their robes and ermine, the Commons of England in their sober garments: the whole council of the nation in an un-dreamed of slaughter.

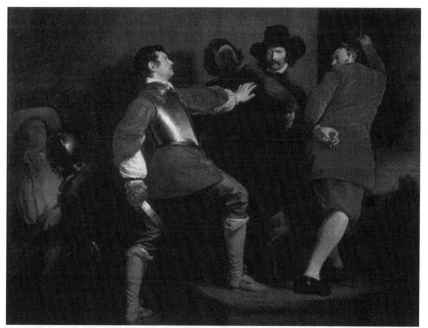

*Fawkes being arrested in the cellars of Parliament, following
the search by the Lord Chamberlain*

We can see now why it is Guy Fawkes we burn. At that
moment of time, on the night of fate, it was he who stood at the
door of the vaults, to be seized by the urgent hands of the
guards and held in firm grasp as the light of the torches
flickered dimly on the high vaulted roof, and the barrels came
one by one to the view of the horrified onlookers. Guy himself,
courageous and defiant, did nothing to mitigate the horror.

 In his pocket were found slow-match and touchwood; by his
own instant confession he had been ready to do the deed which
would have shocked the conscience of the civilized world. Nor
did he express one word of doubt or contrition. On the contrary,
his one expressed regret was that he had not there and then set
light to the powder, going in one moment of time to meet his
maker, together with his captors and the seat of the government
which he loathed and detested.

Taken at once to Whitehall, he confessed his own actions without scruple or remorse. He faced the King whom he would have slaughtered with a steady mien, steadily refusing to say one word to implicate those others who were, for the moment, safe, and who, rather than he, had first devised this fiendish plot. Until the last, it seems that he refused, even under the agony of torture, to divulge anything, before it was already discovered, which could lead to their undoing. His steadfastness at this lonely moment, his courage and endurance, is in strange contrast with the evil he intended. We can feel a stir of wonder and admiration, even as we may shiver with the recollection of the horror, which was contemplated. His courage, however, was in vain. Cecil already knew too much. Now the hunt was well and truly up. Even Catesby accepted that he must run. One after another, the plotters who were in London took to horse and galloped off, apart from Francis Tresham, who boldly stayed put. ,

In spite of everything, one has to admire the stubborn courage of the plotters who refused to admit defeat. The way to the ports was open, but it was to Warwickshire that the conspirators first turned their horses. Rookewood's fast stable took him there swiftly, so that he passed the others on the road. That anyone with pretensions to sanity could have believed in the possibility of a successful revolt with such a handful of leaders seems incredible; perhaps they hardly believed in their own mad undertaking.

The first destination was Dunchurch, where Sir Everard Digby was holding his "hunting party" in readiness to seize the Princess Elizabeth. The party was gathered, and with sublime confidence or insane folly Digby explained what was to have been done, inviting his guests to join the standard of rebellion. As might have been expected, he was greeted with angry denunciations, and the plotters, with their servants and personal followers, again took to horse and made off for Warwickshire. Neither sense nor experience seems to have influenced them;

even now they had not given up hope of leading a revolt, and they appealed right and left for support. Predictably, they had no success. To make matters even worse (if possible) they committed the further folly of stealing horses on the way, so that a hue and cry was raised before the news of the unhappy plot could arrive from London.

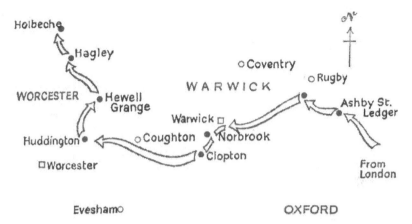

The escape route from London to Worcestershire

The sheriff of Warwickshire chased them to the borders of the county, where the sheriff of Worcestershire took up the pursuit. When they reached Huddington, Winter's house, they were visited by Father Tesimond, who said Mass and then departed on the futile errand of trying to raise help in Lancashire. From Huddington, with dwindling support, they moved to Holbeche, the home of Humphrey Littleton, one of the few Catholics to join in the mad enterprise.

Holbeche, the home of Humphrey Littleton

Here there occurred an accident in which even the conspirators saw the hand of God. In their bedraggled and weary state, after the long journey through the winter countryside, they found that their supply of powder had become wet. They spread it near an open fire to dry it out; a spark fell upon it, and exploded it. Several of the plotters were badly injured, and the spirit of the others was crushed. Robert Winter, Digby, and the servant Bates departed, though they were all taken later.

Dunchirch, where the plotters first assembled after their escape

When the sheriff of Worcestershire attacked, the remaining handful decided to die fighting with their swords. It was a miniature massacre. Both the Wrights, Catesby and Percy were killed; Thomas Winter was badly wounded and taken prisoner, together with Grant and Rookewood. Keyes, who had left them after Dunchurch, was taken later. Within a few days, all the conspirators were either dead or in custody.

CHAPTER 6 – The Reach and The Halter

In those days, trials were something of a mockery. The prisoner was accused by learned and skilled advocates, but had to defend himself as best he might, without skill and without a full knowledge of what would be brought against him. It was for the prisoner to prove his innocence-if he could! Probably he was tortured, and a written confession extorted from him in his agony was quite likely to be falsified afterwards.

Some of the prisoners had been tortured, notably Guy Fawkes himself. When we are reading about this period and the age which had preceded it, we come across the word' 'torture" so often that we are apt to forget the horror which is implied. Good men, kindly generous men who, in their private lives, were given to works of charity, seem to have felt no pang as they stood beside the rack, and watched victims writhe in agony, or listened to their pitiful cries as they lay sweat covered and mutilated. When we are thinking about the wonder of honest men plotting butchery, we must not forget that a people who are governed cannot be expected to excel their governors in morality or truth. It is a lesson we still have to learn.

Fawkes, as we have said, had been brutally tortured, and he came to his trial a pitiful wreck in body, yet still strong in spirit. We call it a trial by courtesy; but what we would now call a trial was then unknown. At the best, the prisoner was allowed to prove his innocence, denied of skilled help, and often without knowing exactly what it was of which he was accused. In this case there could have been no defence, whatever had been the system of so-called trial. Guy Fawkes had been caught red-handed, and he must pay the penalty. His companions were mostly little better off.

Guy Fawkes being tortured by the rack

All the prisoners except Digby pleaded not guilty, though they made it clear that these were formal pleas only. As one of them put it: better be convicted than convict oneself. The point in doubt was how they were to be put to death. Incredible though it may seem, the brutal custom of the day was thought inadequate by some, and a commission actually sat to consider what might be done. In the end, the routine method of the day for traitors was adopted: hanging, drawing and quartering. The details of this barbarous procedure are really too horrible to describe in detail. Suffice it to say, the prisoners were drawn on hurdles to the place of execution, being unfit to tread the same ground as ordinary men. There they were partially hanged, and then mutilated in an unspeakable way whilst still alive. When death finally came, it must have seemed the most merciful moment of their lives.

The extraordinary thing is that even the victims seem to have taken this frightful punishment philosophically. It was quite usual for he who condemned and he who suffered to dine together the night before, as Drake did on his famous voyage with an officer he had condemned. This is the sort of thing we have to realize if we are to try to understand the age we are dealing with.

In this case there was no dining together; some would have been in no state to dine with anyone. But the condemned men upon their scaffolds made speeches to the crowd who had come to see the gruesome tragedy enacted. As they prepared to die they confessed their guilt and asked pardon. In this solemn moment we might have expected innocent men to have protested their innocence, whatever the convention of their age. Not one of them did so.

Epilogue

WHAT is the truth about the Gunpowder Plot? It is often suggested that the whole thing was a wicked plot of Cecil's, but this is hard to believe in the light of what we know. The plotters themselves did not deny their guilt; some of them seem to have gloried in it. Of course it could be argued that they hoped for mercy right up to the last moment, but this does not seem very likely! It has been argued that Thomas Winter's confession, which was fairly full and frank, was extorted under torture, and is therefore valueless. It has even been claimed that this confession was a forgery. It is signed with the name Winter, though at all other times he signed as Wintour. It is also said that his arm, which had been damaged during the fight at Holbeche, would have prevented him from writing.

Certainly there are grounds for some suspicion. There is no doubt that the confessions were altered. One can say that it would have been fully in keeping with Cecil's cunning to have engineered the whole plot, in the sense of having used agents provocateurs. Remembering the Babington plot, one can even imagine his puckish humour providing for the vault to be conveniently untenanted, or even supplying the plotters with powder. There are few lengths to which he might not have gone. But how far would this have freed the prisoners from guilt?

In the Genesis story of the Garden of Eden, God did not hold Adam blameless because Eve tempted him. If a crime is committed or attempted, it is not to be excused, whatever the circumstances. And if the confessions were indeed bogus, there are two important things left unexplained.

Door to Little Ease prison cell at the bottom of the White Tower in the Tower of London. The cell is 4 feet square to prevent any person from standing up or lying down. Guy Fawkes was kept in Little Ease for a day before being put on the rack.

In the first place, some of Digby's letters were smuggled out of the Tower, and were found many years later among his son's papers; in these, which were not seen (and were not meant to be seen) by official eyes, he makes no attempt to hide his guilt, and is only hurt and puzzled because his actions have been so misunderstood. He is sad and surprised to find that his fellow Catholics censure him rather than praise him.

Secondly, the prisoners can have been in no doubt about their fate when they were dragged to the place of execution on hurdles and knew that they were about to suffer a horribly painful death. In those days, condemned men were allowed to address the watching crowd before the grisly work was done. Not one of them denied the facts, nor claimed that there had been any misrepresentation. However far Cecil may have gone in encouraging the plot and faking evidence, it seems impossible to believe that the conspirators were not willing tools. They were blamed bitterly, not least by their fellow Catholics, and they accepted the blame. There seems no doubt whatsoever that Cecil knew about the plot. His spy system was excellent, and apart from Fawkes all the men concerned were so well known to him as "security risks" that he must surely have had at least a fair idea of what was going on. Indeed, he admitted as much. When Lord Monteagle brought him the anonymous letter, he said that he had knowledge of a plot of some sort connected with the opening of Parliament. His behaviour is quite understandable if he had merely a general idea of the plan, but not nearly so easy to interpret if he knew the full story, so that the claim that he organized the whole conspiracy does not seem to be at all convincing.

A yeoman gaoler of the Tower

The Babington plot has been cited as an example to show how
the Government, and in particular the Cecils, father and son,
were willing to lead plotters on. Yet, if examined carefully, the

earlier plot is evidence against the younger Cecil's having detailed knowledge of the Gunpowder Plot. In the case of Babington, there was no elaborate charade involving bogus exposure and reluctant investigation; the Government merely waited until the right moment, and then pounced. Why, then, the pretence of reluctance and disbelief in the Gunpowder Plot, unless the uncertainty were genuine? By staying his hand until so late, Cecil might well have given the conspirators a chance to escape. Being the sort of man he was, he would not willingly have given them the opportunity.

There is another very small point. When Fawkes had been taken, a proclamation was issued denouncing the traitors, and naming Percy as the leader. This would be natural in a state of partial ignorance, since the vault had been hired in Percy's name; but why should the wrong name be given if Cecil knew the real leader? Why was the original list inaccurate? It has been claimed that since the manufacture of gunpowder was a Government monopoly, the plotters would have been unable to obtain a vast store of it without Cecil's connivance. But this is surely a minor point. Powder was available in large quantities for the private arms, which were the legitimate property of most of the gentry, and for widespread use for firearms used in sport.

On the other hand, there are grounds for thinking that one or several people involved may have been spying for Cecil. Monteagle himself, who was apparently given a pension of £700 a year by a grateful Government, is heavily suspected.

With his past record, it is hard to believe that Cecil and the King would have treated him with the fulsome praise and flattery which was accorded him merely because he handed over the letter. Percy and Tresham are other possibilities, it has been suggested, but if so then they would presumably have drawn back before their own wives were forfeit and if Tresham had been in Cecil's service, he would have made himself out to be an eager plotter instead of a rather reluctant one. In point of fact, almost anyone might have been a spy; but if so, then we are back at finding Cecil's behaviour hard to understand. The question of the anonymous letter is harder still to unravel, and has been a favourite historical mystery ever since.

Almost everyone who has studied the matter suspects Monteagle of having had a hand in it. True, his behaviour was in some ways suspicious. His sudden resolve to go to Hoxton has been much commented upon, though nobody can make out why it was so important for him to receive the letter there rather than anywhere else. Moreover, he deliberately gave it to Ward to read aloud. If he had wanted an excuse to show it to someone who would warn the plotters, he could not have chosen better.

What has not been sufficiently explained is why he should arrange for a letter to be written to himself. If he were in the plot, and wished to betray it, he could have done so quite easily by the simple method of warning the conspirators and then tipping off the authorities. If we assume that the letter was genuine so far as he was concerned, the only problem is to account for the way in which he was treated by the Government. There were great efforts made to keep his name out of the whole matter during the trial, and even some of the confessions were altered so as to omit his name whenever he was mentioned.

If the whole episode of the anonymous letter had not been rigged by Monteagle, either on his own or with Cecil, then who was the author? The plotters themselves suspected Tresham, and charged him with it. The fact that he apparently succeeded in persuading them that he was not guilty goes some way to proving that he was telling the truth. On the other hand, his whole conduct, and that of the Government, looks highly suspicious.

Part of the Tower of London.

When the others fled, Tresham remained calmly in London. He was not arrested until sometime after the others, though he was there ready to hand. Most suspicious of all is the fact that he died "of natural causes" in the Tower before he could be brought to trial. Naturally, it has been claimed that he was poisoned because he could tell too much. Perhaps he did die of poison; but what could he have known that he could not be allowed to reveal? That Monteagle had been in the plot, and had ratted? But in that case the others would have known, too. No very good explanation has ever been offered.

There remains the dull possibility that the letter was genuine; that it was sent by someone who either wanted Monteagle to be saved, or else wished to thwart the plot without revealing his identity. It is not inconceivable that Father Garnet could have been responsible; if his conscience troubled him, he might have chosen this way of saving the situation. Even Ann Vaux could have sent it. In fact, almost anyone might have done, and we shall never know the truth.

Since so many eminent historians dismiss the simple explanation, perhaps we must be content with a belief that there was "dirty work at the double-cross roads", and amuse ourselves by trying to think up more and more ingenious theories! There are two postscripts to the story. The first is the trial and execution of Father Garnet, who was charged and convicted, though he was granted the "mercy" of being allowed to hang until he was dead. Over this trial, controversy rages more violently than ever. Of what, if anything, was he guilty? Certainly it was admitted that he had been told all about the plot under the seal of the confessional. The real question was whether he knew also by other means, and failed either to reveal the plot or to do his best to scotch it. To this question there is no definite answer, though when he was on the scaffold he admitted that he knew of the plot and had not denounced it. Since he did not claim that he knew of it only under the seal of the confessional, there are grounds for thinking that he had found out in a way that would have enabled him to take action without betraying his sacred calling.

Fathers Gerard and Tesimond escaped; but Tesimond had undoubtedly consorted with the plotters at Huddington after their treachery had been shown up, and Gerard too must come under some suspicion.

One particularly sad and strange aspect of the whole story is the venom and energy with which modern Catholic writers attempt to clear the plotters in general, and the Jesuits in particular, of being involved in a plot of which some of them were certainly guilty. The Society of Jesus has a record over the years and over the breadth of the world which needs no defence against the charge that a handful of its members, at one time and in one place, were guilty of errors of judgment and of condoning a cruel and evil plan. If the whole controversy could be cleared of partisan and passionate feelings, we would be more likely to arrive at a just appreciation of what really happened. We might even feel a certain kind of sympathy for the men who, under great provocation, felt themselves driven to a plot which was undoubtedly to be a case of "the end justifying the means". Moreover, they behaved with courage even when faced with horrible and painful death.

The second postscript is in the way of a moral-even if this is a highly unfashionable ending to a story. The whole plot was aimed at securing tolerance for the Catholic faith. In pursuit of what they believed to be a good objective, the conspirators were prepared to use what they themselves knew to be evil means. As history so often shows, evil means are seldom successful even if the intentions are honest. Far from securing greater tolerance, the result of the great plot was a violent surge of anti-Catholic feeling, and a severe tightening of the laws which restricted them. Even the possibility of an atmosphere in which the modern idea of tolerance might have been given a chance to take root was postponed for over a century. In failing, the Gunpowder Plot brought sorrow and suffering to the very people whom it had been meant to help. We can only conjecture; but it is as certain as anything in this uncertain world can be that if the plot had succeeded the lot of the Catholics would have been even worse.

83474517R00038

Made in the USA
Middletown, DE
11 August 2018